LITERATURE ACTIVIT
for
YOUNG CHILDREN

Art Projects • Skill Building Activities • Plot Summaries

BOOK 1

Written by Diana Sullivan

Illustrated by Nedra L. Pence

Table of Contents

Teacher Created Materials, Inc.
P.O. Box 1040
Huntington Beach, CA 92647
©*1989 Teacher Created Materials, Inc.*
Made in U.S.A.
ISBN 1-55734-300-4

Introduction

Literature Activities for Young Children employs a multi-sensory approach to learning based on twelve popular children's books. This book incorporates a variety of activities to meet the needs and learning styles of young children. Many follow-up suggestions are listed and include the following:

(1) Extended Activities

- finger plays
- games, songs, and poems
- creative movement
- field trip suggestions
- choral reading
- jump rope rhymes
- questioning techniques
- gross motor activities
- dramatic play
- show 'n' share ideas

(2) Art Activities

- stencils
- puzzles
- fingerpainting
- mosaics
- salt dough
- sponge/bleach/candle paintings
- paint blowing
- pinata
- wax crayon rubbings
- tissue overlays

(3) Seatwork

- mazes
- counting
- matching sets to numerals
- sequencing
- categorizing
- hidden pictures
- rhyming
- dot to dot
- tracing
- upper and lower case letters

Special Note:

Because some art projects in this book may present too much coloring for young children, the following options may be helpful.

- Outline the character.
- Color only certain items, e.g. the hat and shoes; specify which colors to use.
- Duplicate pattern pieces onto colored construction paper.
- Have children work as a group to complete one project.
- Glue fabric scraps, paper, glitter, beans, etc. to decorate a project.

The Story About Ping

By Marjorie Flack and Kurt Wiese

SUMMARY

Ping is a duck who lives in a boat on the Yangtze river. Everyday Ping and the other ducks are let off the boat to hunt for snails, fish and other foods. In the evening all the ducks are expected to board the boat quickly. The last duck on the boat always receives a swat on the back with a stick.

One day, Ping is not paying attention when all the other ducks are boarding the boat. He knows he will be the last duck to board the boat. Ping, not wanting a swat on the back, hides in the bushes until the boat sails away. He then begins lots of adventures on the Yangtze river with fishing birds and an encounter with a family on a house boat where he almost loses his life. Ping escapes the houseboat and heads for his duck family's boat. He once again is the last duck to board the boat, but this time chooses the swat on the back. He is just so happy to be home with his duck family again.

SUGGESTED ACTIVITIES

Buttermilk And Chalk Duck Painting: Xerox the duck outline shape (page 9) onto white construction paper. Cut the duck shape out. Keep your colored and white pieces of chalk separate. Fold some wax paper in half. Put the pieces of chalk (all the same color) inside the wax paper. With a hammer, crush the pieces of chalk. Spread buttermilk completely over the duck paper. Add one small pile of colored chalk (or white chalk) to portions of the duck. Rub the chalk pieces into the buttermilk on the duck paper. Add other small piles of colored or white chalk to different portions of the paper. Try mixing two colors of chalk.

Duck Rhythm Movements: (children imitate)

a. duck *waddling* and *quacking*

b. duck *pecking* at insects, snails, frog (duck's food) on the ground

c. duck *building a nest* and *laying eggs*

d. duck *swimming* and *diving* for fish

e. duck *pecking* its way out of an egg

Duck Sculpture: Make a clay duck.

Pet Store Clerk or Visit a Pet Store: Invite a pet store owner to visit your classroom or plan a field trip to a nearby pet store.

The Lost Duck

1. Use your crayon to help the duck find his way to the ship.

2. Color the picture.

Family Fun

1. Draw a picture of Ping and his family on the water.

2. Color.

Food for Ducks

Color the foods that a duck would eat.

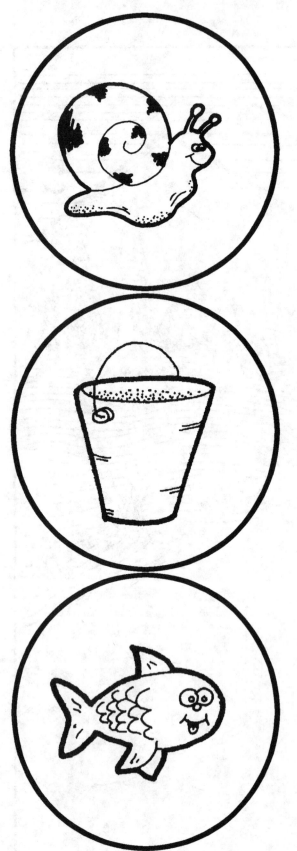

Chinese Kite

Read the word and color.

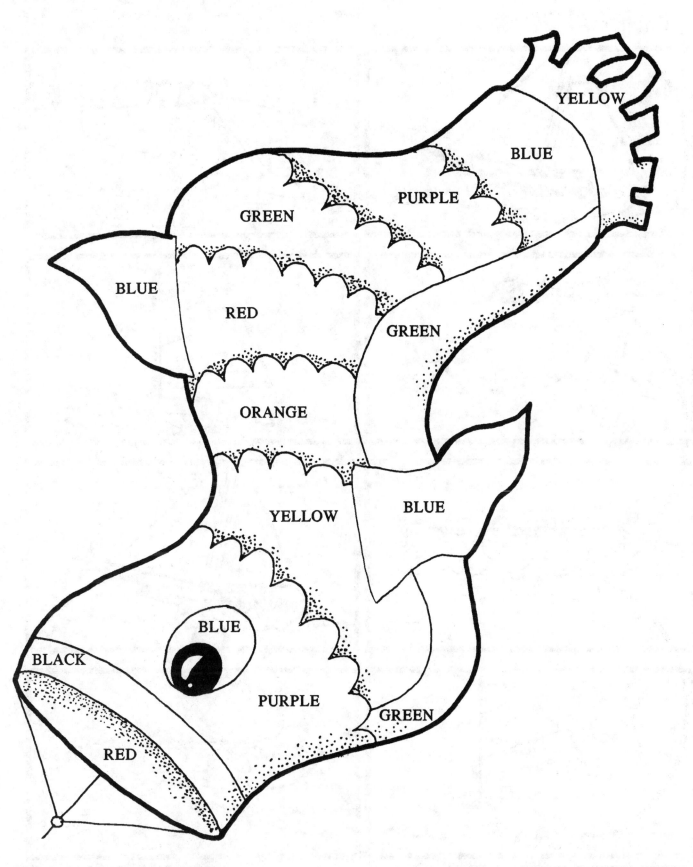

Match the Color

1. Match the boats.

2. Color.

Name _____

The Story About Ping Activity

* See suggested activity page 3.

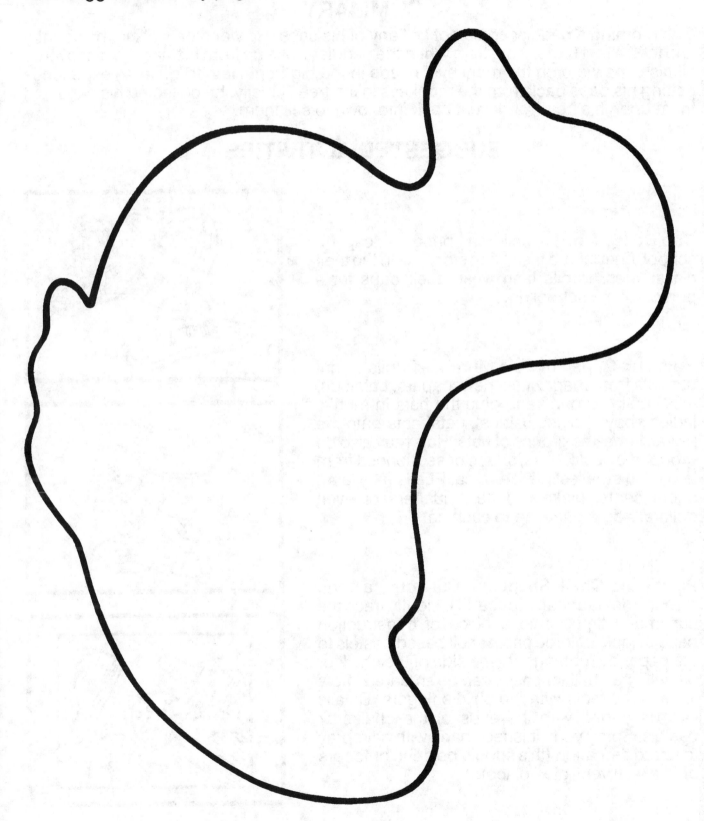

Caps For Sale

By Esphyr Slobodkina

SUMMARY

One morning a peddler could not sell any of his caps. He went for walk in the country and took a rest under a big tree. When the peddler woke up from his nap, he discovered all his caps were on the monkeys' heads in the big tree! He had quite an experience getting his caps back from the monkeys in the tree. Finally, he collected his caps, put them upon his head, and went back into town to sell them.

SUGGESTED ACTIVITIES

Cap Collection: Children bring a cap to school. They share their "cap story" with the their classmates. Pupils then wear their caps for a portion of the school day.

Hats and Caps For Sale Mural: Pupils cut out hats from magazines, newspapers, catalogs, etc. Pupils "group" and glue the hats in men's, ladies', boys', girls', babies', pets' hats onto the mural. Label the groups of hats. Hats may also be grouped by color, size, shape or sequenced from largest to smallest or vice versa. Pupils may learn about cents, nickels, dimes, quarters or even dollars. Add a price tag to each hat.

Pastel and Chalk Shapes: Cut out a cap stencil from tagboard (page 11). Lightly trace the cap many times onto a piece of construction paper. Apply colored chalk or oil based pastels to the paper by rubbing with the side of the chalk or pastel. The chalk or pastel can be smeared into a variety of effects with the child's fingers. Details can be added with the ends of the chalks or pastels. Spray your finished shape with hairspray to retard smearing (this should be done outdoors or in a well ventilated place).

Name _____

My Hat

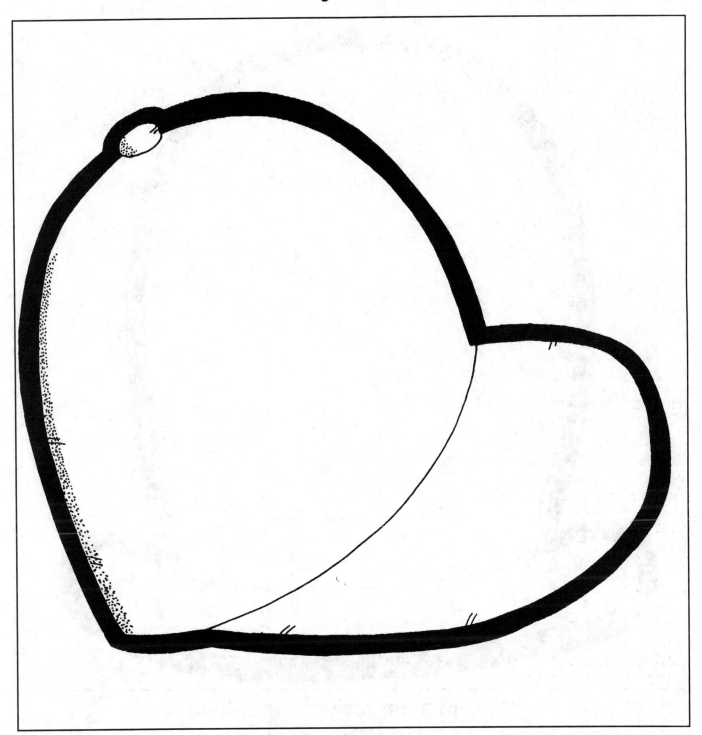

Design a hat yourself!

1. Decorate your hat using designs from page 13.

2. Color your hat.

3. Share your hat with the class and tell where you could wear it.

My Monkey's Hat

Design a hat for your monkey!

1. Decorate the hat using designs from page 13.

2. Color the hat.

3. Now, share your monkey's hat with your class and tell where he could wear it.

Hat Decorations

Name _____

Caps For Sale

Matching Caps

1. Match the caps.

2. Color each pair of caps the same.

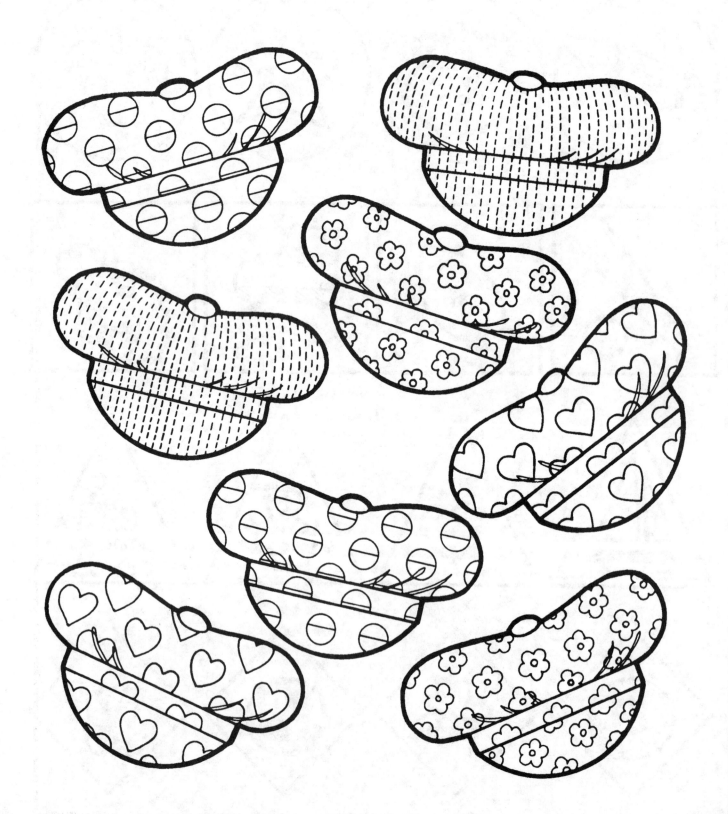

Name _____

Hidden Hats

1. Find the hidden hats.
2. Circle them and color the picture.

Madeline

by Ludwig Bemmelmans

SUMMARY

Madeline lives in a home in Paris with eleven other little girls. They dress alike, eat the same thing, and go on outings together. They do everything together!

One night Madeline is rushed to the hospital to have her appendix out. She has a wonderful hospital stay with lots of flowers, toys, candy and a visit from the other eleven little girls she lives with.

That evening, back in the home, the eleven little girls begin crying in their beds because they, too, want to have their appendix out and have a fun hospital stay like Madeline's.

SUGGESTED ACTIVITIES

Flower Painting: Have children paint a large picture of a flower on butcher paper. They can experiment with mixing primary colors into secondary colors and making color hues by adding white or black paint. Extension: Children may create his/her own paint color by mixing the colors of paint.

Flowers Finger Painting: Have children draw several flowers in a finger painting art project.

Hand Painted Flowers: The children cut out stems and leaves from green construction paper and glue the parts of the flower onto white construction paper. The teacher pours paint into the bottom of a pie pan. Children press their flattened out left and right hands into the paint and then print them onto the top part of the stem. The child's hand print forms the flower. Varieties of colors of handprints add interest to this project.

Doctor or Nurse Visitor or Visit to a Hospital: Invite a doctor or nurse to visit your classroom or plan a field trip to a nearby hospital.

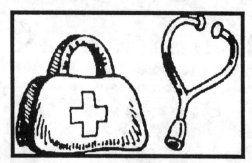

Flower Yarn Shapes: Draw a simple flower outline with a black marker or crayon on white paper. Place a sheet of wax paper on top of the flower paper. Make a glue solution of half water and half household glue. Dip colored yarn into the solution. Form the glued yarn over the flower design, on top of the wax paper. Let the glued yarn flower dry overnight. Lift the flower up the next day. You will see a colored yarn outline of a flower.

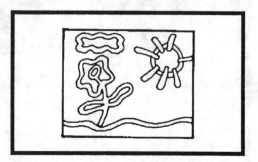

Balloon Match

Match the set on the balloon to the number.

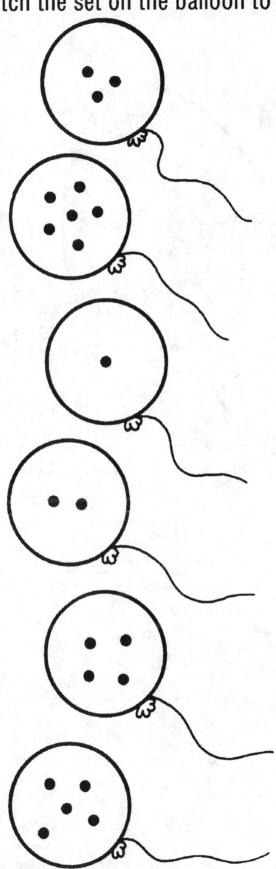

5
2
3
6
1
4

Rain, Rain, Go Away

Connect the dots.

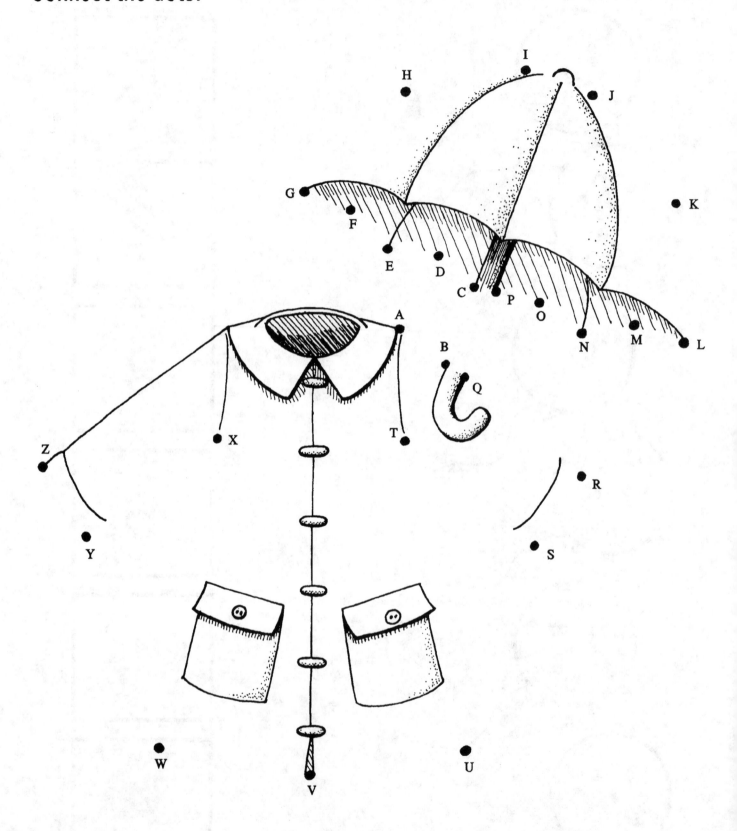

Go Togethers

Match the things that go together.

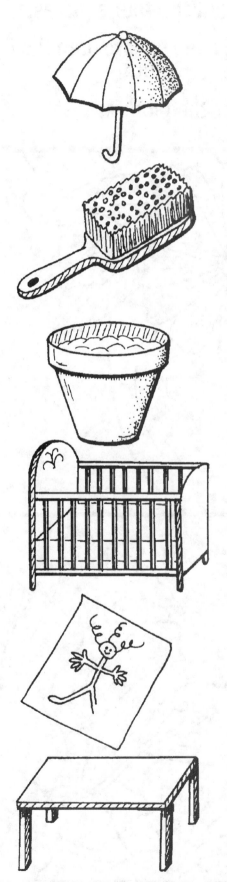

Name _____

Madeline

A Get-Well Bouquet

1. Cut out the four squares.

2. Glue each square onto the frame (page 21), to make a picture.

3. Color the picture.

A Get-Well Bouquet (Cont.)

Paste the picture squares here.

Color The Flowers

1. Trace the lines in the correct crayon color.

2. With watercolors, paint the flowers the correct colors.

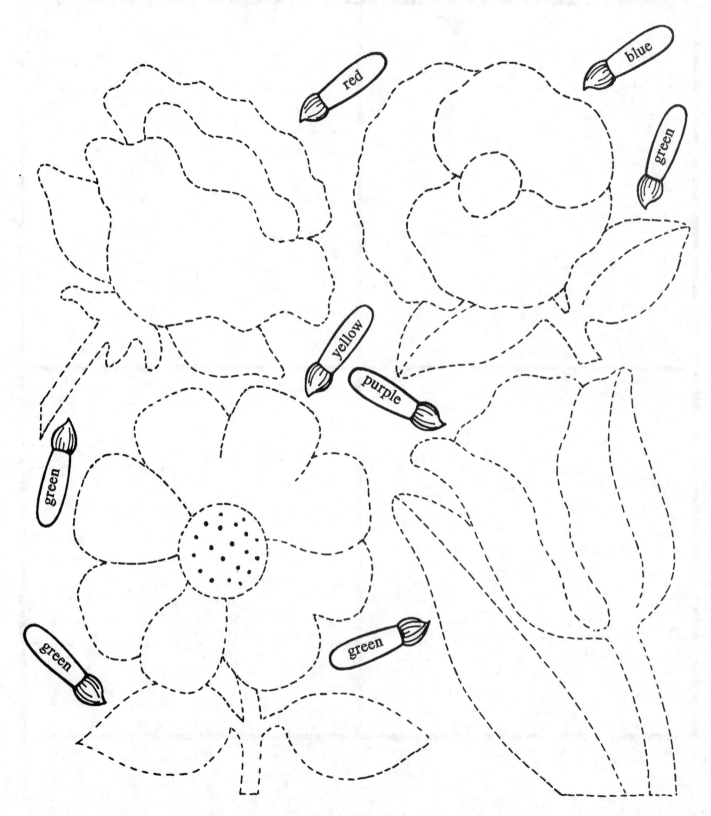

Goodnight Moon

by Margaret Wise Brown

SUMMARY

A little bunny gets into bed for the night. The sky is just beginning to get dark. He says "goodnight" to all the things he sees in his room. The sky is now very dark. He says "goodnight" to all the things outside his window. He then falls fast asleep.

SUGGESTED ACTIVITIES

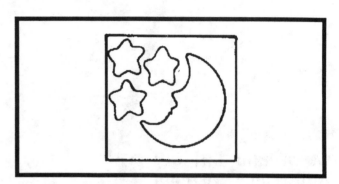

Moon and Stars Silhouette: Make a yellow moon and blue stars (patterns on pages 24-27) out of colored construction paper. Glue the pieces onto a sheet of black construction paper.

Rhyming Pairs: Pupils fold a 9" X 12" piece of colored construction paper into four parts. Then cut out two pictures from magazines, newspapers, catalogs, etc. that rhyme. Glue the two rhyming pictures into the first square. Repeat this process for all the squares. Both the front and back squares of the construction paper can be used.

Graph Paper Shapes: Outline a shape (see patterns on page 24) onto a piece of 1 inch graphing paper. Child cuts out the shape and then colors the 1 inch squares. Try patterning the 1 inch squares for a variety of looks.

Moon and Other Shapes: Supply the children with a variety of colored construction paper (see patterns on page 30-31). The children then attach a shape to an object in the room that contains that shape. For an extended activity, provide the children with a variety of shapes (variations in size and color) and have the children glue the shapes to colored construction paper (in any position) creating a shape design art project. Shrink the shapes on a copy machine for smaller sizes.

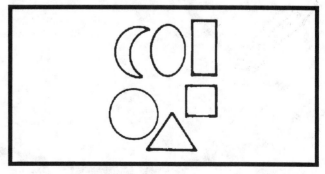

Starry Night

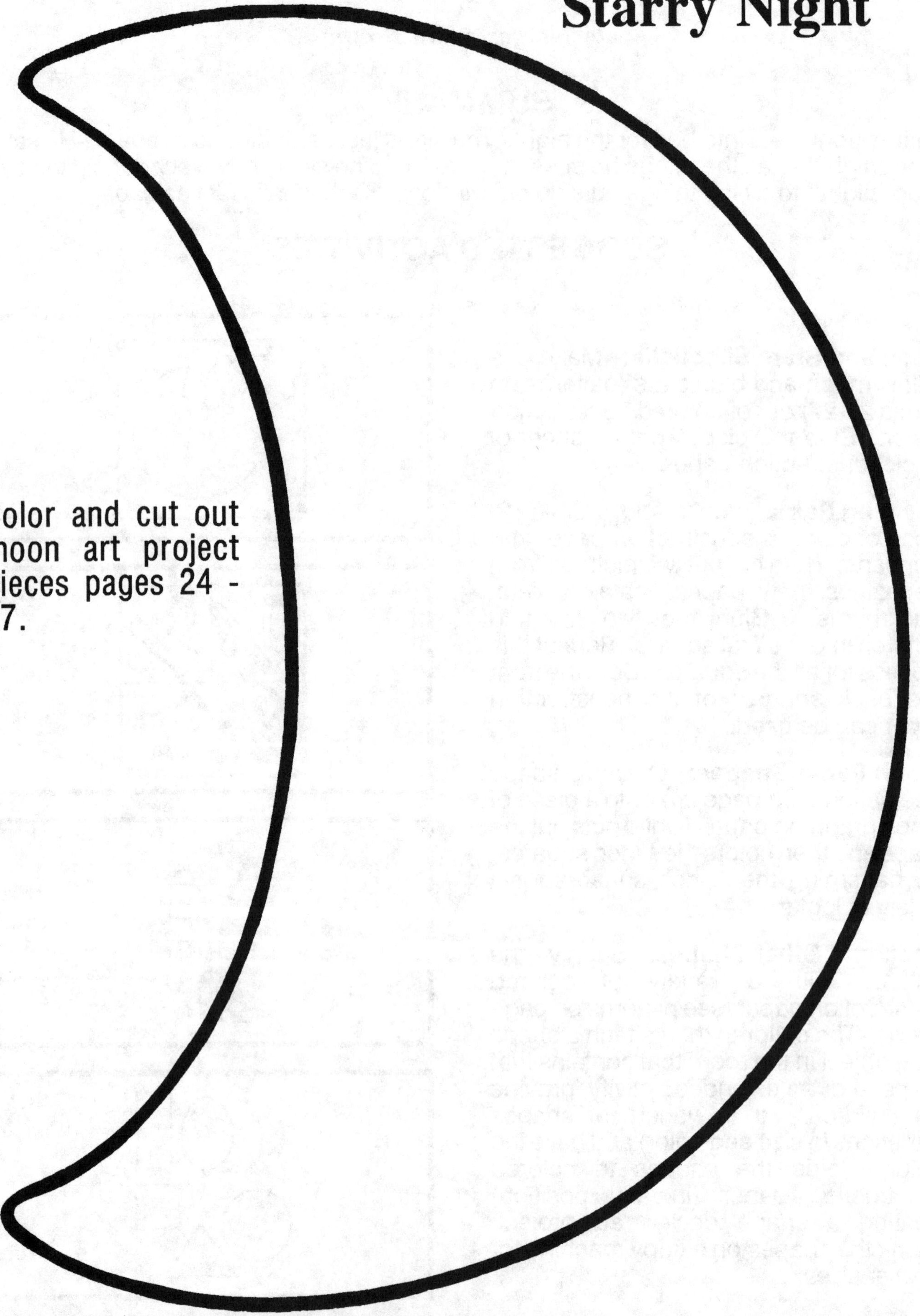

Color and cut out
moon art project
pieces pages 24 -
27.

Goodnight Moon

Starry Night

Star background: Glue Tab A to Side A.

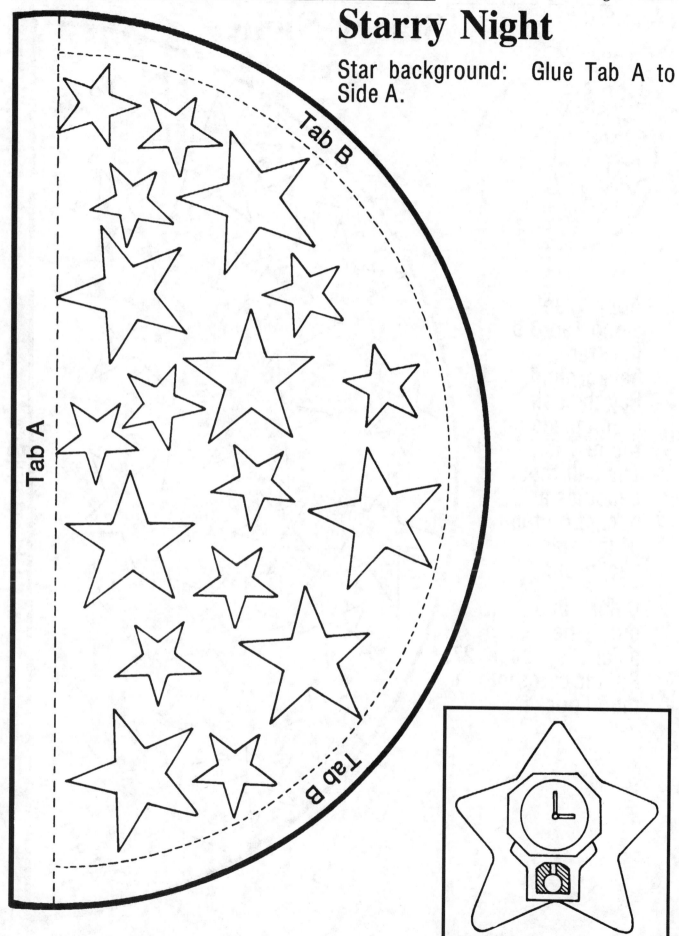

Starry Night

1. Apply glue along Tab B of the star background. Lay the half moon piece on top of Tab B. The half moon becomes a pocket on top of the star background.

2. Color and cut out the card pieces on page 27. Put the cards into the moon pocket.

Name _____

Starry Night

1. Here are some things you could tell good night.
2. Color and cut out the pictures.

Rhyme Time

1. Cut and paste the things that rhyme.
2. Color the pictures.

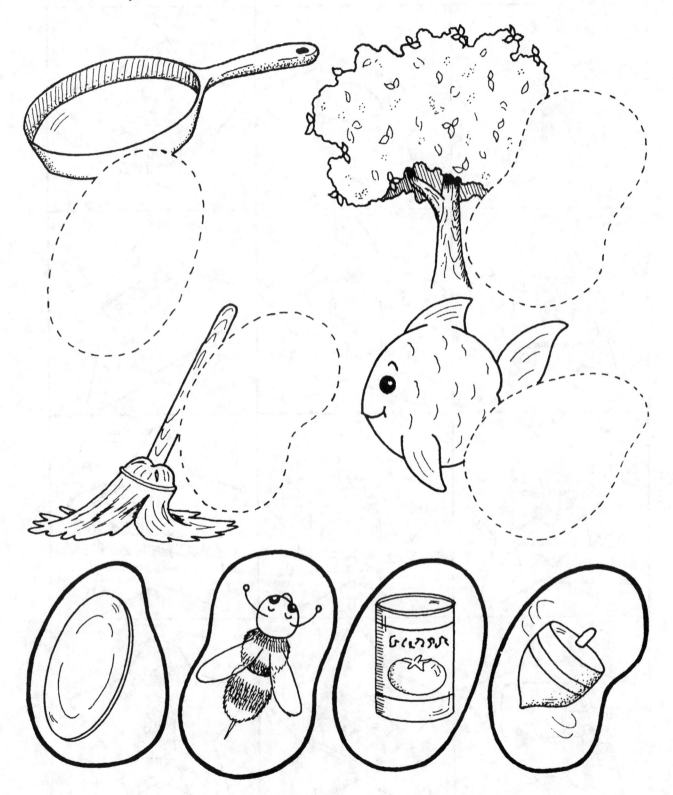

Follow That Path!

Make a path by coloring the things in a bedroom that you could tell "good night."

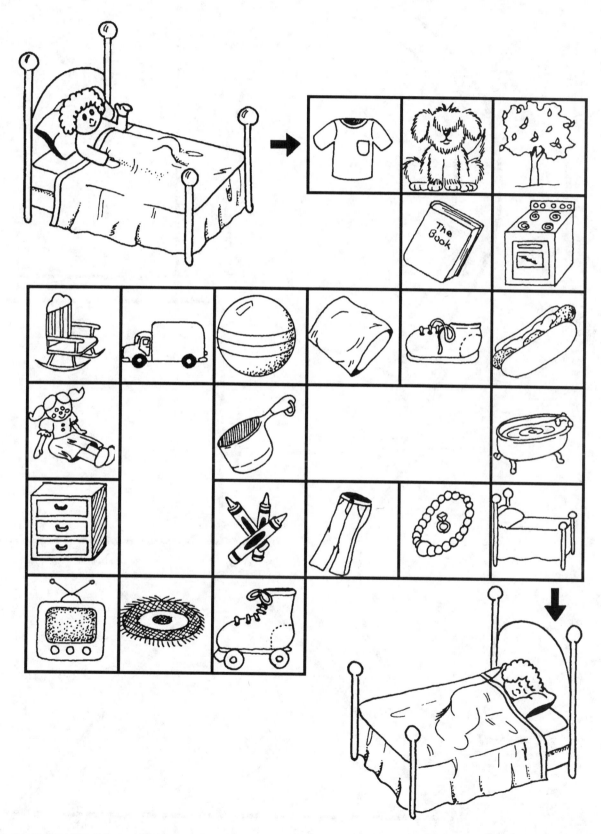

Name _____

Art Patterns

* See suggested activities page 23.

Art Patterns

* See suggested activities page 23.

Nana Upstairs, Nana Downstairs

by Tomie dePaola

SUMMARY

Every Sunday afternoon Tommy visits his grandmother and great-grandmother. Since Tommy's great-grandmother is bedridden in the upstairs part of the house, he calls her Nana Upstairs. Tommy witnesses how his grandmother takes care of his great-grandmother by fixing her food, combing her hair, helping her to sit upright in a chair, helping her in and out of bed for nap times. Tommy calls this grandmother Nana Downstairs.

Tommy has a warm and loving relationship with each of his grandmothers. Tommy's great-grandmother then passes away, leaving the upstairs bed empty. Eventually, his Nana Downstairs ends up in bed, just as Nana Upstairs, and she, too, passes away.

SUGGESTED ACTIVITIES

Grandparents Memory Book: Child draws a picture of a special memory or event that he/she experienced with a grandparent or a great-grandparent. The teacher then writes a sentence or two below the picture describing the event. Each child may make several pictures and combine them into a construction paper book which he/she then gives to his/her grandparent or great-grandparent. Pictures in book may be drawn over several days. Use crayon, colored markers, watercolors, oil pastels, or chalk.

Sequence Strips: Have a group discussion on the aging process of humans. Discuss an elderly person's needs (e.g. help with food, dental attention, walking, seeing, hearing, etc.) Have children cut pictures of people out of catalogs, magazines, newspapers, etc. and sequence the pictures from babies to elderly people.

Name _____

Nana Upstairs, Nana Downstairs

Grandma's Apron

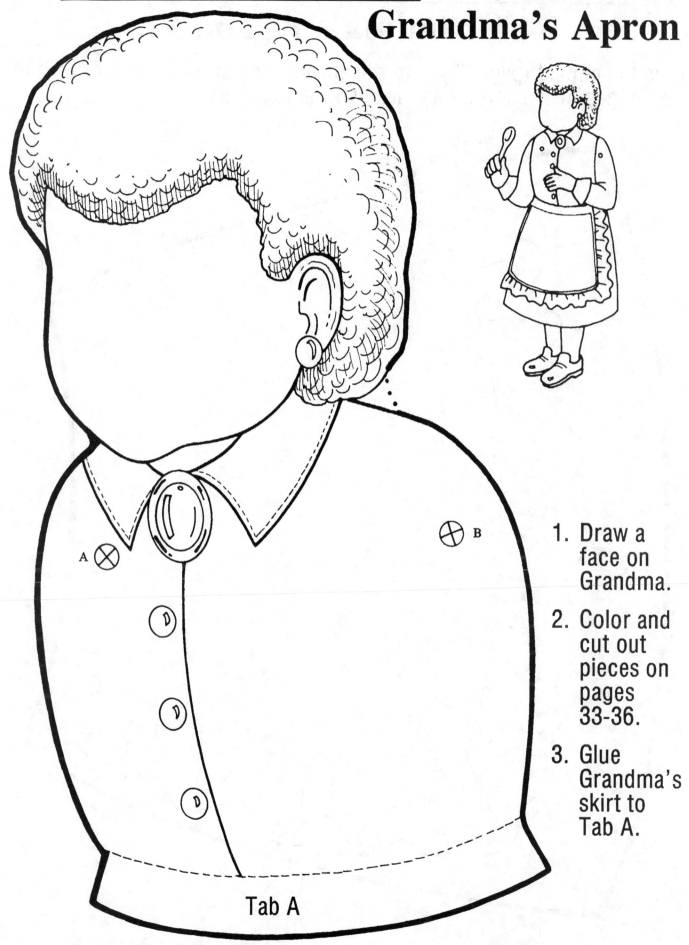

A ⊗

B ⊗

Tab A

1. Draw a face on Grandma.

2. Color and cut out pieces on pages 33-36.

3. Glue Grandma's skirt to Tab A.

Grandma's Apron

Glue the pocket (page 35) onto the apron. Glue around the bottom and side edges of the apron only, leaving the top open.

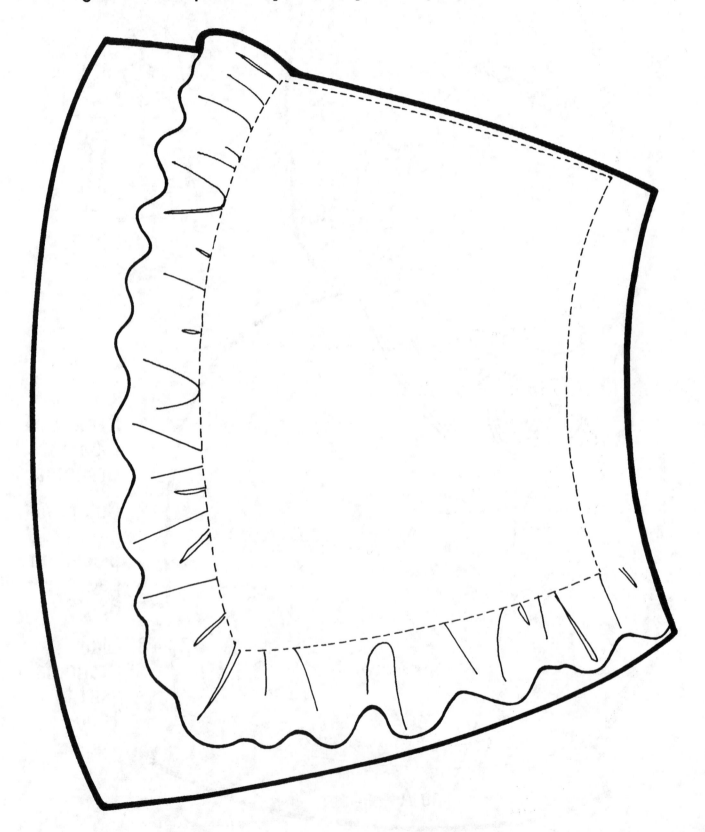

Nana Upstairs, Nana Downstairs

Grandma's Apron

pocket
apron

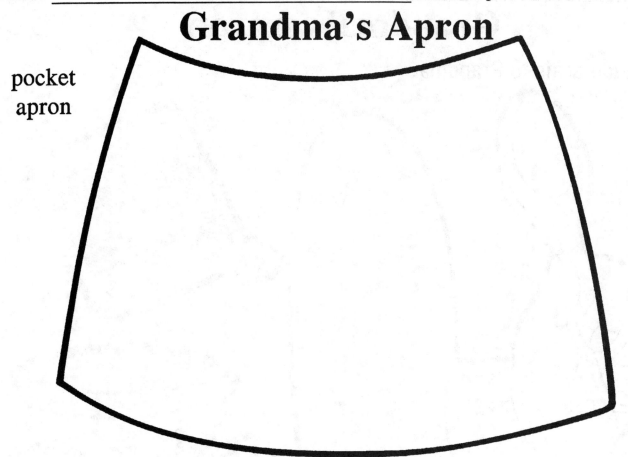

Glue the feet, Tab B, to the dress.

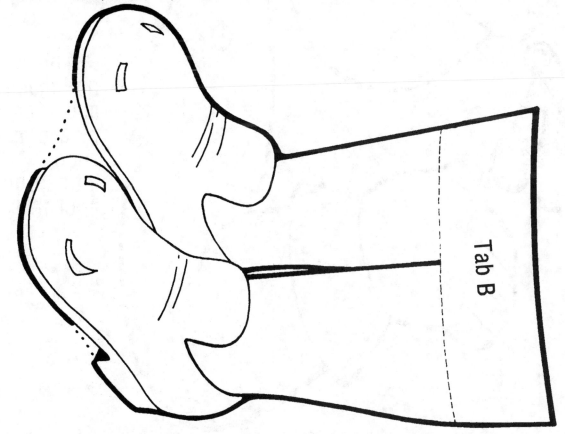

Tab B

Grandma's Apron

1. Attach arms to Grandma.

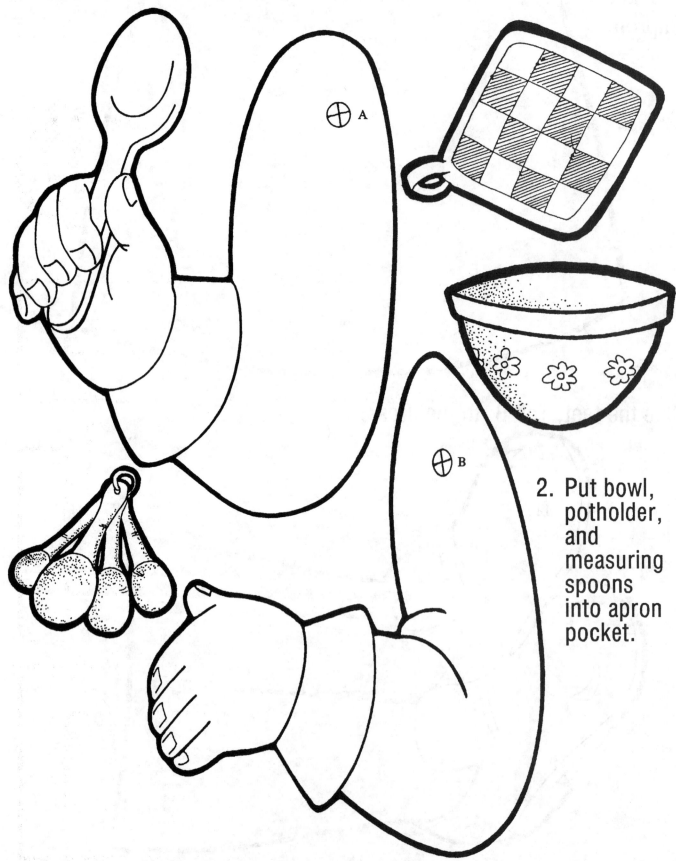

2. Put bowl, potholder, and measuring spoons into apron pocket.

Name _____   *Nana Upstairs, Nana Downstairs*

Grandma's Cookies

1. Find your way to Grandma's cookies.

2. Color the pictures.

Start

My Hair

Color, cut out and paste the pictures in order.

C. Now my hair is brushed.

B. Brushing my hair.

A. Before my hair is brushed.

Lyle, Lyle, Crocodile

by Bernard Waber

SUMMARY

Lyle is a very friendly, helpful and loving crocodile. He experiences many adventures in the city such as playing children's games, cooking, feeding birds, shopping, ice skating and putting on a performance of an old stage act. The city residents complain about a crocodile living in a city, so Lyle is sent to the zoo where he is very unhappy. He is rescued from the zoo by a friend. While driving back to the city, Lyle notices a burning building and rescues the residents. The city dwellers are so grateful to Lyle they invite him to live in their city once again.

SUGGESTED ACTIVITES

Reptile Jigsaw Puzzles: Cut out a large picture of a reptile; glue to tagboard and let dry. With a black permanent marker divide the picture into jigsaw pieces. Then cut the picture apart on the lines. Store the puzzle pieces in an envelope.

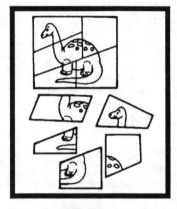
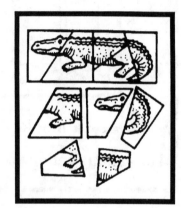

Hide 'N' Seek: Play games of hide 'n' seek. Make it more challenging by having the children count by two's, five's, or ten's.

Jump Rope Activities: Play a jump rope game such as "Over the Brook." Place two jump ropes six inches apart on the ground. Have the children line up; one at a time they must jump over the brook. On the next round, increase the space between the jump ropes. To play Circle Jump Games, place the jump rope in a circle on the floor. Direct pupils to:

1. Jump into the circle, then jump out of the circle.

2. Hop into the circle two times, etc.

Fire Prevention: Discuss fire prevention, fire safety rules, fire fighters and their duties. Invite a fire fighter to visit the classroom or plan a field trip to a fire station.

Lyle, Lyle, Crocodile

How Many?

Complete the pictures.

Draw a monkey in each cage.

How many monkeys are there? _____

Draw a piece of cake on each plate.

How many pieces are there? _____

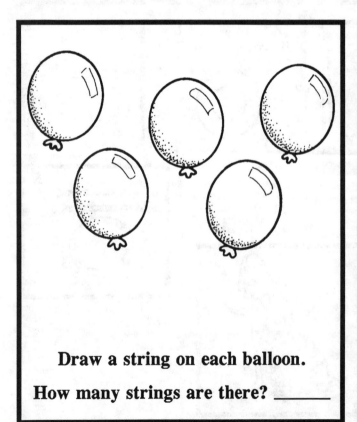

Draw a string on each balloon.

How many strings are there? _____

Draw a scarf on each snowman.

How many scarves are there? _____

Turtle Brad Projects

Color and cut
out egg and
turtle on pages
41 and 42.

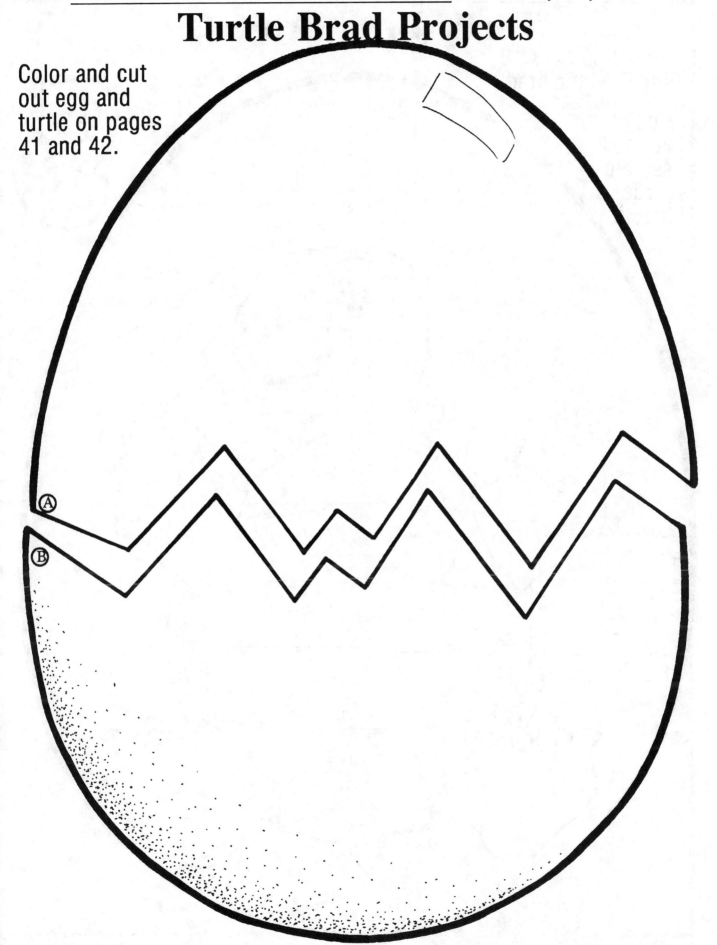

Ⓐ

Ⓑ

Turtle Brad Projects

1. Attach points A, B, and C with a brad.

2. Open the egg to see the turtle hatch.

One Is Different

Put an X on the one that is different in each row. Color the ones that are alike.

Name _____

They Hatch From Eggs

These reptiles hatch from eggs: turtles, alligators, snakes, lizards, and dinosaurs.

Circle one and draw and color a picture of it in the terrarium.

Name _____

The Dinosaur Is . . .

Color, cut and paste.

helpful	friendly	playful

45   #300 Literature Activities for Young Children, Book 1

Name _____

Lyle, Lyle, Crocodile

Guess the Reptile!

Connect the dots and
answer the riddle.

Color.

I can swim.

I have a hard shell.

I can pull myself into my shell.

I am a _____ .

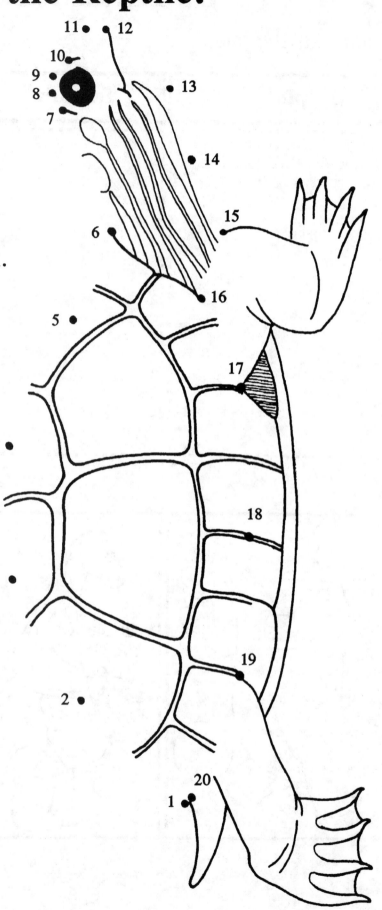

The Little Engine That Could

by Watty Piper

SUMMARY

A little red engine is carrying a load of toys and good foods to the other side of the mountain. Her engine quits and she cannot complete the task. A toy clown from the red engine asks The Passenger Engine, The Big Engine and The Freight Engine to take them over the mountain. The engines decide they are too important, proud, strong and tired to complete such an unimportant task. Along comes a little Blue Engine who has never done an important job. He agrees to take the toys and foods over the mountain. The train builds up his courage to complete this task with the famous phrase, "I think I can."

SUGGESTED ACTIVITIES

Wash-off Paint Engine: Lightly trace the train pattern (page 54) with a pencil onto a sheet of white typing paper. Outline the tracing with thick white poster paint. Dip a piece of sponge into the thick, white paint and "stamp" a texture inside the engine outlined in white paint. Let the paint dry thoroughly. Paint over the whole sheet of paper with India Ink, covering up all the dried white paint. Let the picture dry thoroughly. Dip the picture into a sink or pan full of water. The white paint and some of the ink will wash off. The engine outline will appear through the ink.

Yarn Engine: Duplicate the train pattern (page 54) onto tagboard. Cut out the engine shape. Mix one teaspoon of wallpaper paste into a half pint of cold water and let stand for fifteen minutes. Soak a long piece of black yarn in the paste mixture; gently squeeze off the excess paste from the yarn. Outline the engine shape and make two windows on the engine in black yarn. Then fill in the engine spaces with long pieces of yarn that wind around the engine's shape until the whole engine is completely covered.

"Engine Number 9" Jumprope Rhyme: Beall, Pamela and Susan Nipp. *Wee Sing And Play*. California: Price/Stern/Sloan Publishers, Inc., 1986 (page 42).

"The Little Blue Engine" Poem: Silverstein, Shel. *Where The Sidewalk Ends*. New York: Harper And Row, Publishers, Inc., 1974 (page 158).

Helping Others: With the children, discuss the importance of helping others. Point out that:

- You can be young, old, little or big to help others.
- Willingness, Positive "I Can" Attitude, Action to do task helps us to help others.
- Have the children tell about some times when they have helped others.

Color and cut out the rectangle pictures on pages (48 - 51). Glue the engine rectangle (page 48) to Tab A (page 49). Glue that rectangle to Tab B (page 50). Glue that rectangle to Tab C (page 51). Fold the rectangles back and forth into an accordion book train.

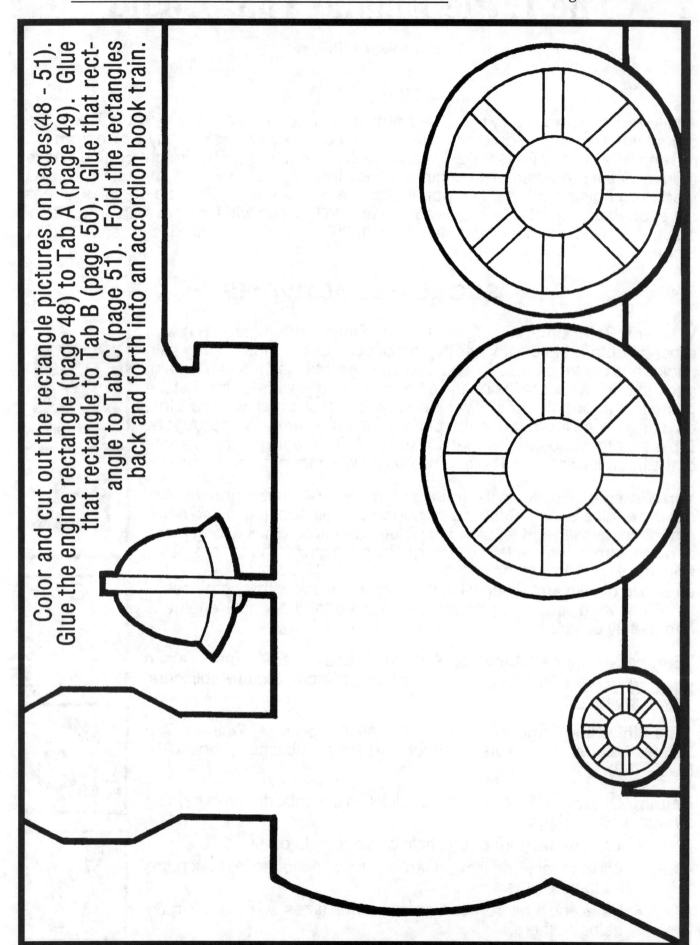

"I think I can . . . ."

Tab A

"I thought I could . . . ."

Tab B

Tab C

The Little Engine Said . . .

1. Find the smoke puffs' message.
2. Color.

"

___
4

___ ___ ___ ___ ___
7   3   8   6   5

___
4

___ ___ ___ !"
2   1   6

Match the Food and Toys

1. Color and cut out the pictures above the line.

2. Paste the foods in the basket below.

3. Paste the toys in the toy box below.

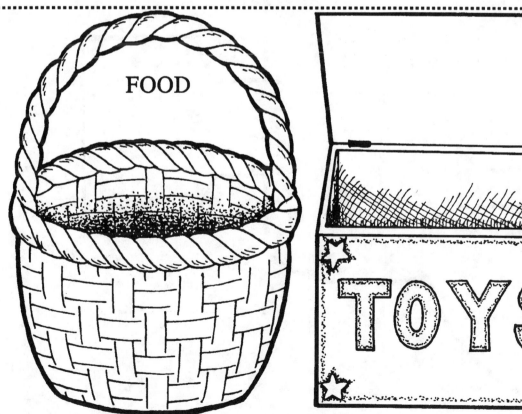

Train Pattern

* See suggested activity page 47.

Little Toot

By Hardie Gramatky

SUMMARY

Little Toot did not like to work, he liked to play on the water. Other little tugboats teased Little Toot for playing when he should be working. Feeling ashamed and angry, Little Toot decided to change his behavior and become a good worker. No one took his many offers to work seriously. This left him sad and lonely until a raging storm brewed up in the ocean. An oceanliner was stuck between two rocks in the raging storm. Little Toot faced his fear of stormy waters and rescued the oceanliner thereby winning the respect and admiration of all the other tugboats.

SUGGESTED ACTIVITIES

Candle Painted Tugboat: Lightly trace the boat pattern (page 60) with a pencil onto a sheet of white typing paper. Outline the tracings with the candle. Press down hard (candle point may be sharpened with a knife to help you trace the tugboat). Add water to some tempera paint, making a thin, watery paint. Paint over the whole sheet of paper with the watered-down paint. The waxed outline of the tugboat will appear through the paint.

Crayon Boat Overlay: Supply each child with a tagboard boat piece (pattern on page 60). Trace the tagboard boat onto a variety of colors of construction paper. Then cut out the boat shapes and glue them into any position on a 9" X 12" sheet of blue construction paper. Fill in the spaces with dots, horizontal or vertical lines, crossed or dashed lines. Use a different color crayon or marker than the colors of the intersecting boats.

Boats Fingerpainting: Have the children draw several boats and waves in a blue fingerpainting art project.

"Homemade Boat" Poem: Shel Silverstein, *Where The Sidewalk Ends.* New York: Harper and Row, Publishers, Inc. 1974 (page 12).

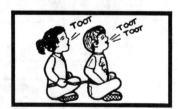

Pretend To Be Tugboats: Pretend you are a tugboat. Sail out into the calm water. Make a circle, oval, wavy lines, zig zag lines, figure-eight in the water. The water gets rougher — rock back and forth; a raging storm overtakes your little boat — sail over the huge waves back to the safe harbor.

Changing Who We Are: Discuss how our actions show others what kind of person we are. Little Toot was a silly tugboat, until one day he decided to show others, through his actions (not his words) that he was going to be a changed person. Discuss how positive action changes in our own personalities or actions can change the way other people "see" us.

Stack and Puff Match
Match the letter partners.

Name _____

Little Toot

Number Names

Match the names to the numbers.

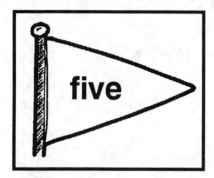

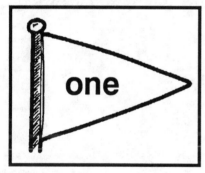

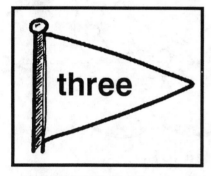

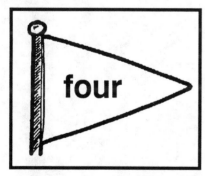

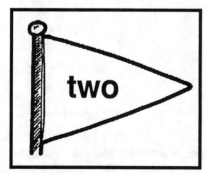

Help!

S.O.S. is a call for help. Trace and color the S.O.S.

Draw a picture of yourself in need of S.O.S. (help).

Your Own Boat

Trace the boat. Draw a flag and a smoke puff. Color.

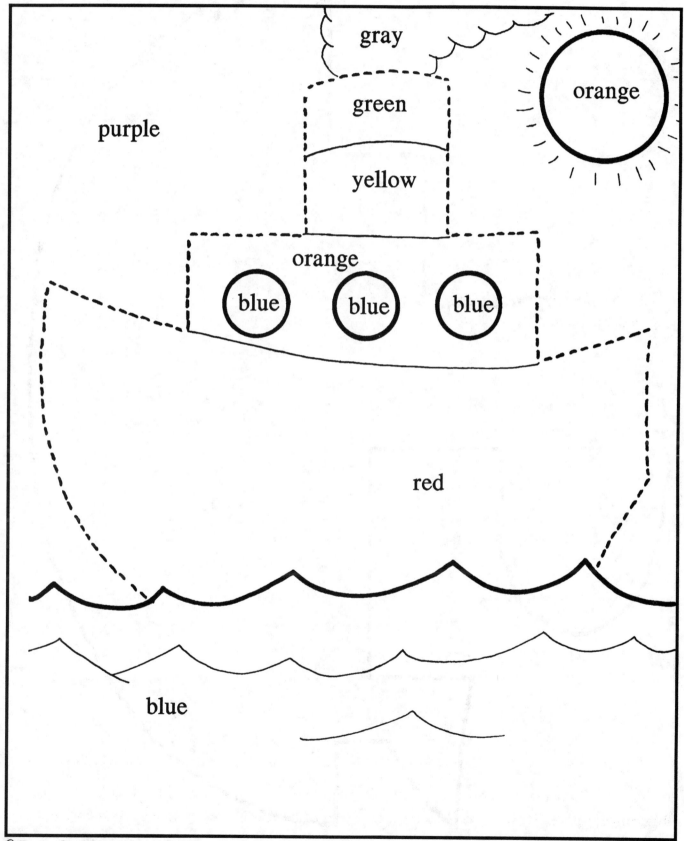

gray

orange

green

purple

yellow

orange

blue   blue   blue

red

blue

Boat Pattern

* See suggested activity page 55.

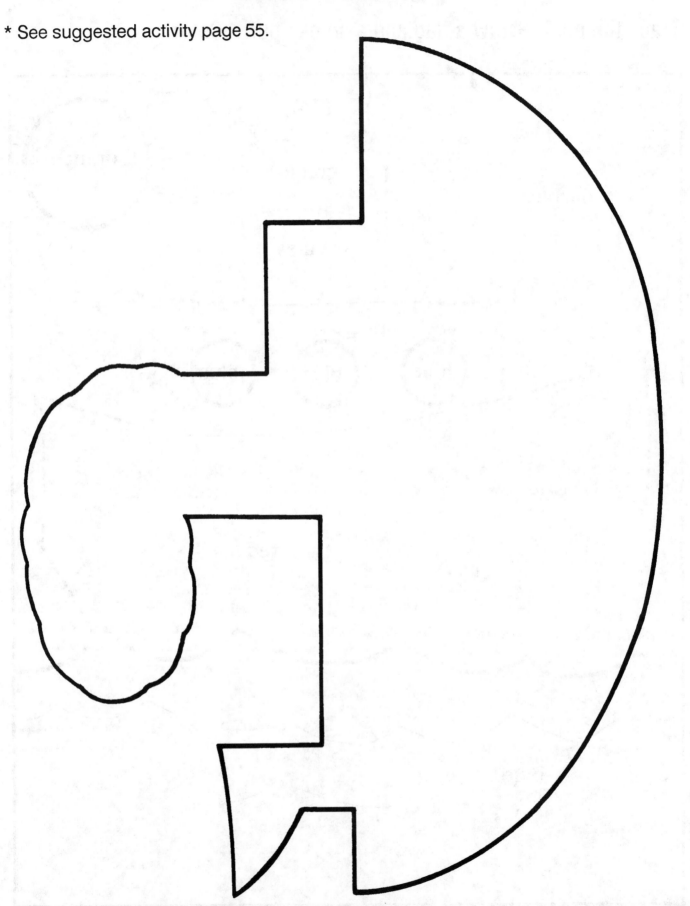

Brown Bear, Brown Bear, What Do You See?

By Bill Martin, Jr.

SUMMARY

This book contains verses that have a chain of characters looking to see who the next one will be. It begins with a brown bear who sees a redbird; the redbird sees a yellow duck, etc. The chain covers the following characters: Brown Bear, Redbird, Yellow Duck, Blue Horse, Grey Mouse, Green Frog, Purple Cat, Pink Elephant, White Dog, Black Sheep, Goldfish, Teacher, and Children.

SUGGESTED ACTIVITIES

Painted Animal Stencils: Make the animal stencils (pages 70 and 71) from tagboard or stencil paper. Mix colors of thick, powdered tempera paints. Place a stencil on a piece of white construction paper. With your paintbrush, paint inside the stencil's cut-out space. Color the animals unusual colors.

Bear Tissue Overlay: Make an outline of a bear on white construction paper. Cut out the bear shape and coat with liquid starch. Layer pieces of yellow and brown tissue paper on top of the starch, overlapping many pieces of tissue (creating darker and lighter tones of yellow and brown). Then let bear dry. With a black permanent marker, draw a face and paws on the bear.

Felt Animals: Use the animal stencils on pages 70 and 71 for patterns. Trace a pattern on a piece of colored felt. With a black felt tip pen or a paint tube of glitter, make the animal's details. Details can also be made with scrap pieces of leftover felt. Put your animals on display on a flannel board.

Choral Reading: Children will enjoy reciting the lines together in this book.

(1) "Brown Bear, Brown Bear, What do you see? I see a _____ looking back at me" (As you turn each page).

(2) "Brown Bear, Brown Bear, What do you see?" _____ (As you turn the page).

SUGGESTED ACTIVITES (Cont.)

(3) "Brown Bear, Brown Bear, _____?"
_____ (As you turn the page).

Animal Shadows: Position an overhead projector to shine on the wall. Have children take turns moving into the lighted area and pretending to be one of the story animals. Their animal shadows will appear on the wall. Have the other children guess which animal is being characterized.

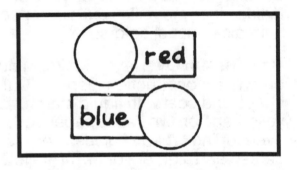

Animal Follow The Leader: All the children line up. The first child imitates an animal as he/she moves around the room. The other children do what the leader does.

Color/Color Word Cards: Make several circles out of colored construction paper. Make one white rectangle for each colored circle. On each rectangle, print the word name of the color using the same color pen, i.e. the word red should be printed in red ink on the white rectangle. Attach rings of masking tape on the back of the cards. Have children take turns matching the cards to same-colored objects in the room.

Clapping Rhythms: Children clap their hands to the repeated verses in "Brown Bear, Brown Bear, What Do You See?"

Brown Bear, Brown Bear, What Do You See?

The Seagull Family

Cut out and glue the pictures in order from the youngest to the oldest.

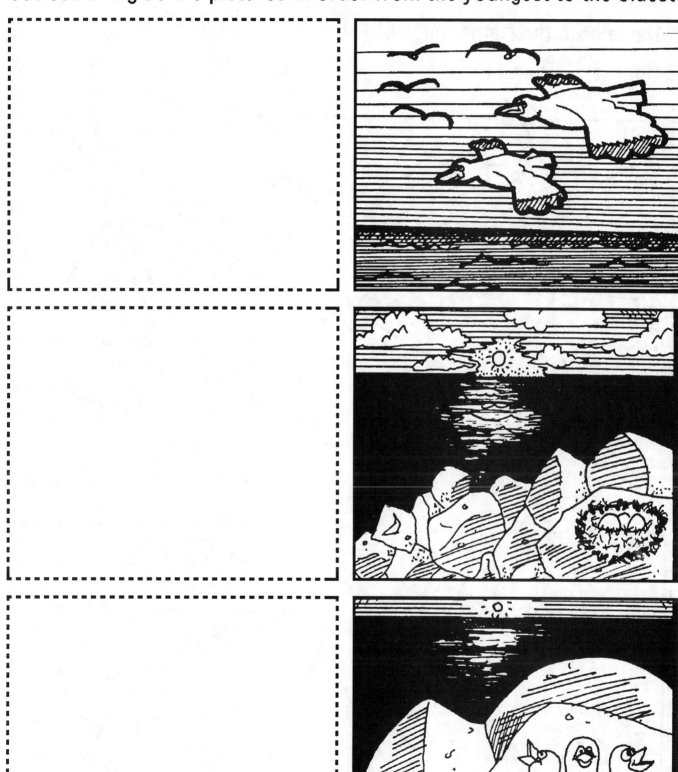

Bear Puzzle

1. Cut out the puzzle pieces.

2. Paste onto the frame (page 65).

3. Color and draw a face.

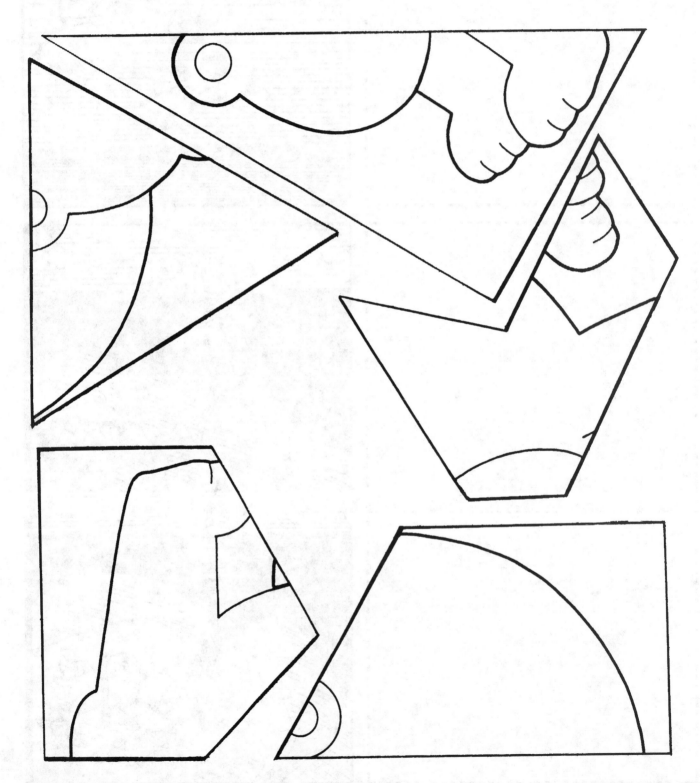

Bear Puzzle

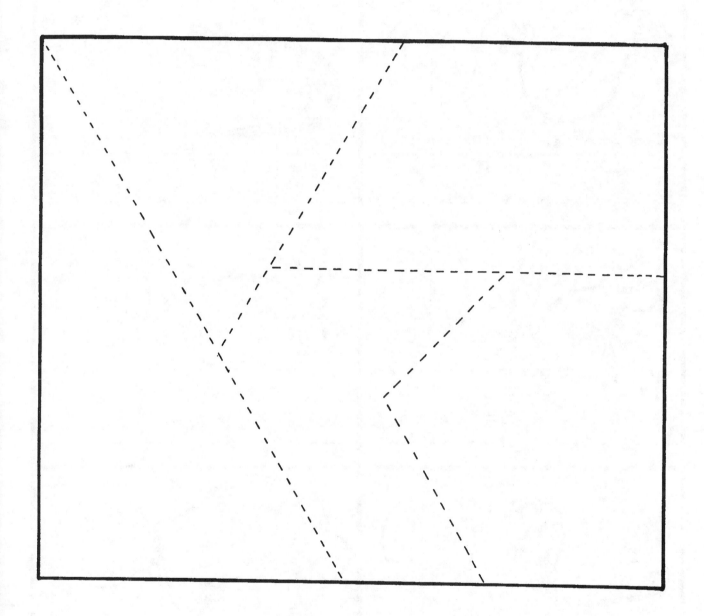

Look At Me!

1. Trace the numbers and number words.

2. Color and cut out the pictures.

3. Glue the pictures in order onto a sheet of construction paper.

Name _____

What Do You See?

Trace and color.

Rainbow Colors

Trace the names and color the rainbow.

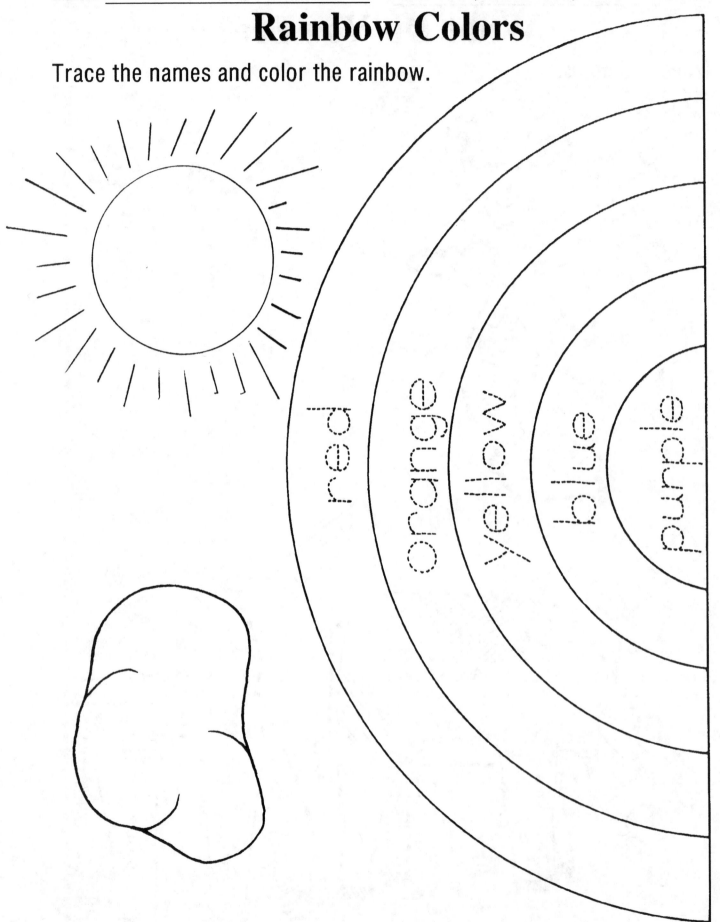

What Did He See?

Brown Bear saw many animals. Color the animals he **did not** see.

Animal Patterns

* See page 61.

Name _____ *Brown Bear, Brown Bear, What Do You See?*

Animal Patterns

* See page 61.

Amelia Bedelia And The Baby

by Peggy Parish

SUMMARY

Amelia Bedelia is asked to babysit although she had no baby-sitting experience. The mother of the baby leaves Amelia a note. Amelia reads and interprets the note literally. She and the baby have many adventures due to her misinterpretation of the note. In the end, Amelia has a successful babysitting experience.

SUGGESTED ACTIVITIES

Baby Paper Collage: Cut out pictures and/or words about babies from magazines, newspapers, or catalogs. Glue the pictures onto a piece of colored construction paper. Fill up the whole page with pictures and/or words, overlapping portions of the pictures.

Baby Eggshell Mosaic: Color eggs using the same method used to color Easter eggs. Peel the shells and put each color into a separate container. Gently break up the egg shells into small pieces. Duplicate the baby pattern (page 77) onto white construction paper. Apply white household glue to a small portion of the baby picture. Sprinkle the egg shells over the glue. Repeat this process until the whole baby picture is covered. Let dry.

Caring For A Baby: Discuss, show pictures and items of the following: (1) the newborn baby, (2) a baby's development, (3) caring for a baby (bathing, feeding, clothes, fresh air and sunshine, sleeping needs, handling a baby).

Babysitting Babydolls: Provide some baby dolls, clothes, combs, brushes, shoes, socks, bottles, toy dishes, etc. Children pretend to be babysitters and must take good care of the babies!

"Miss Lucy Had A Baby" Jumprope or Clapping Rhyme: Beall, Pamela and Susan Nipp. *Wee Sing And Play.* California: Price/Stern/Sloan Publishers, Inc., 1986 (page 40).

"The Sitter" Poem: Silverstein, Shel. *A Light In The Attic.* New York: Harper And Row, Publishers, Inc., 1974, (page 14).

Baby Toys

Connect the dots.

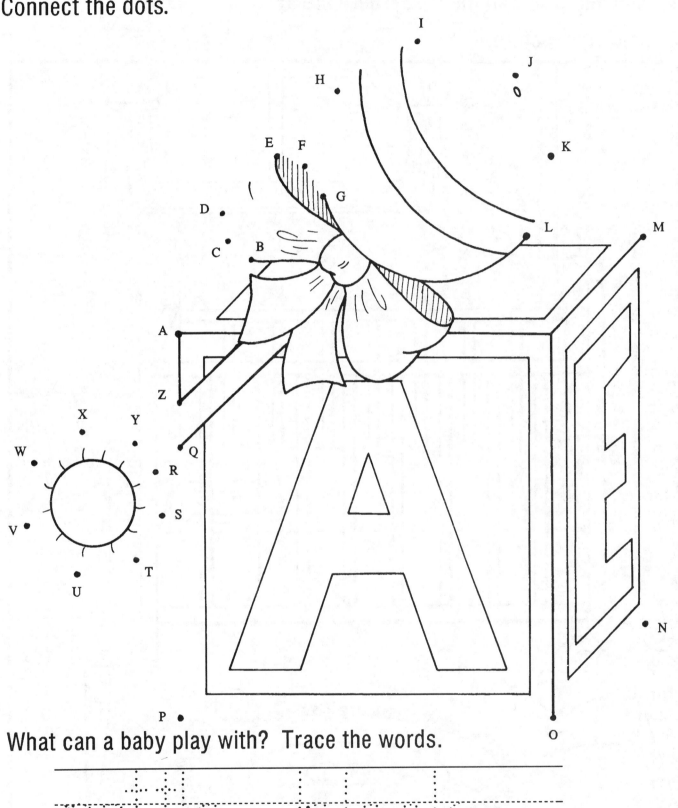

What can a baby play with? Trace the words.

rattle block

Hidden B's

1. Find and circle all the B's. There are 15.

2. Color the picture.

All About Baby

Trace the pictures. Color.

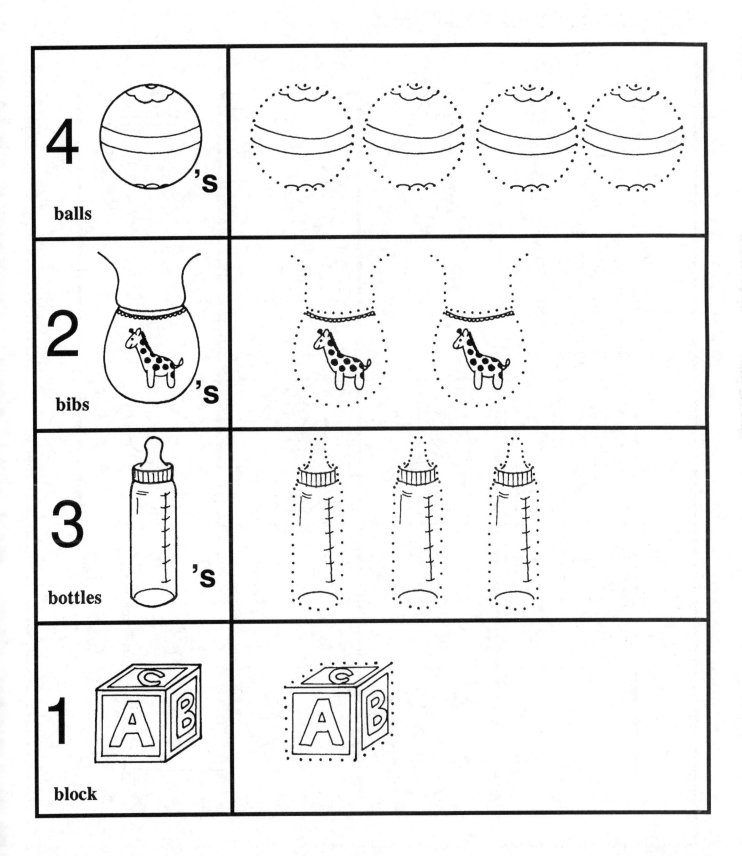

4 balls

2 bibs

3 bottles

1 block

A Baby Needs Many Things

1. Make a path.
2. Color the things a baby needs.

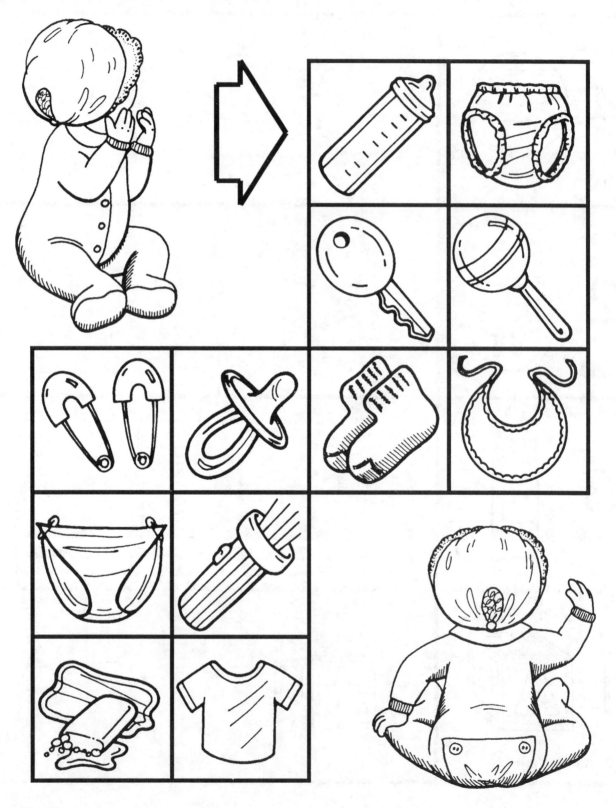

Baby Pattern

* See suggested activity page 72.

Millions of Cats

by Wanda Ga'g

SUMMARY

An old man and an old woman were very lonely and they decided that a fluffy cat would make them happy. The old man went on a journey and discovered a hill where trillions of cats were residing. Unable to choose which cat he liked best, he brought them all home to his wife. But the old couple realized that they could not feed all the cats. They decided to keep the prettiest one. All the cats quarreled over who was the prettiest of their group and in their quarreling ate each other up! Only one scraggly cat remained. He had survived the quarrel by not claiming to be the prettiest cat. The old couple nurtured the scraggly cat and turned him into the prettiest cat they had ever seen.

SUGGESTED ACTIVITIES

Tissue Paper Cat: Duplicate the cat outline shape (page 85) onto white construction paper. Cut circles of yellow and orange tissue paper or napkins. Put dots of glue on the cat (one small section at a time to prevent glue drops from drying). Pinch the center of each circle and then glue this "squished" circle to a dot of glue. Cover the whole cat. Other colors may be used for a background of green grass and blue sky.

Learning About Cats: Talk about and show pictures of the following: breeds of cats; the hair and whiskers; the eyes; the teeth; the paws; grooming a cat; feeding a cat; raising kittens. Bring a pet cat to show the children. Let the children play with and cuddle the cat.

"The Lost Cat" Poem: Silverstein, Shel. *A Light In the Attic.* New York: Harper And Row, Publishers, Inc., 1974 (page 151)

"Drats" Poem: Silverstein, Shel. *Where The Sidewalk Ends.* New York: Harper And Row, Publishers, Inc., 1974 (page 72)

Salt Dough Cats: Make a salt dough mixture. Make a cat.

Dancing Movements to Songs: Children can dance to songs about cats. Let them dance to the music moods and rhythms.

Pet Store Field Trip: Visit a pet store and learn about the animals in there.

Name _____

Find the Cats

Millions of Cats

Help the children find the cats.

Guess the Pet!

1. Connect the dots.
2. Color.

I have long or short hair all over my body.

I have sharp claws and teeth.

I purr when I am happy.

My eyes shine in the dark.

I am a

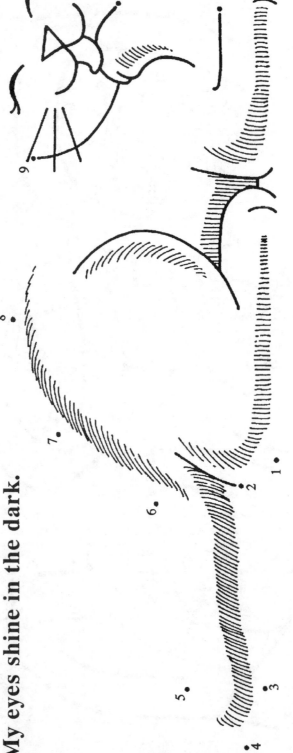

What Do Cats Like?

Color all the things a cat likes.

Basket Full of Yarn

1. Color and cut out the balls of yarn on page 83.

2. Choose the pictures that rhyme with cat and paste them in the basket.

3. Color the basket.

Name _____

Basket Full of Yarn (Cont.)

Trace and Match

Trace the numbers. Then match the numbers to the pictures.

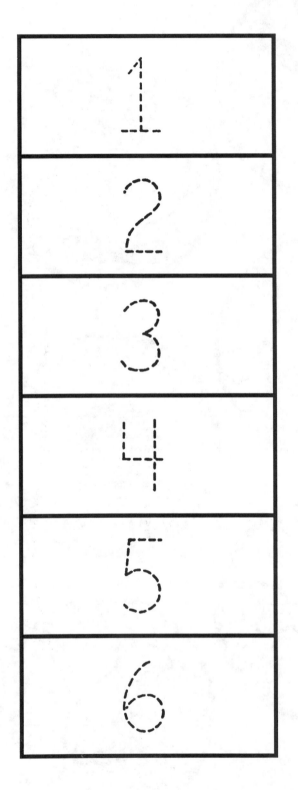

Cat Pattern

* See suggested activity page 78.

Dandelion

by Don Freeman

SUMMARY

Dandelion is invited to a "come as you are" party. Dandelion decides to become more stylish for the party with a haircut, shampoo, manicure, new hairstyle, new jacket, cap and cane. When he arrives at the party, his hostess Jennifer Giraffe does not recognize him and closes her door to him. As Dandelion waits outside Jennifer's door, the weather ruins his new hairstyle and clothes. He ends up looking like his usual self. Once again he knocks at Jennifer's door. This time she recognizes him and invites him inside to join the party. Dandelion decides to always be his plain self from then on.

SUGGESTED ACTIVITIES

Paint Blown Lion: Duplicate the lion outline (page 87) onto white construction paper and cut out. Place some globs of watered down tempera paints or water color paints onto the lion paper. With a straw, blow into the paint, moving the liquid paint color all over the lion figure. This process may also be done with watered down globs of ink.

Lion Pinata: Papier mâché over a balloon. Let dry. Paint the papier mâchéd balloon yellow. Let dry. Add black features (eyes, nose, mouth, whiskers) with marking pen, construction paper or felt pieces. Add tissue paper mane. Cut a small hole in the top of the lion head pinata and stuff the inside cavity with peanuts, little toys, and pieces of wrapped candy. Pupils take turns hitting the pinata with a bat or stick while being blindfolded. When the pinata breaks, pupils pick up the treats and little toys.

"This Is Not Me" Party: Dress up in old clothes or costumes. Come to this party as a make believe person.

I Am Special Just As I Am!: Talk about: (1) physical likenesses/differences (height, weight, eyes, hair, skin color, feet/hand sizes, features, etc.); (2) things we like/do not like to do; (3) places we like/do not like to go; (4) food we like/do not like to eat; (5) what we want to be when we grow up; (6) places we like to travel to; (7) favorite toys; (8) school subjects we like/do not like; (9) family members; (10) family pets, etc.

Best Dressed Lion

1. Color and cut out lion.

2. Color and cut out the clothes on page 88.

3. Glue the clothes onto the lion.

4. Draw shoes on your lion.

Best Dressed Lion (cont.)

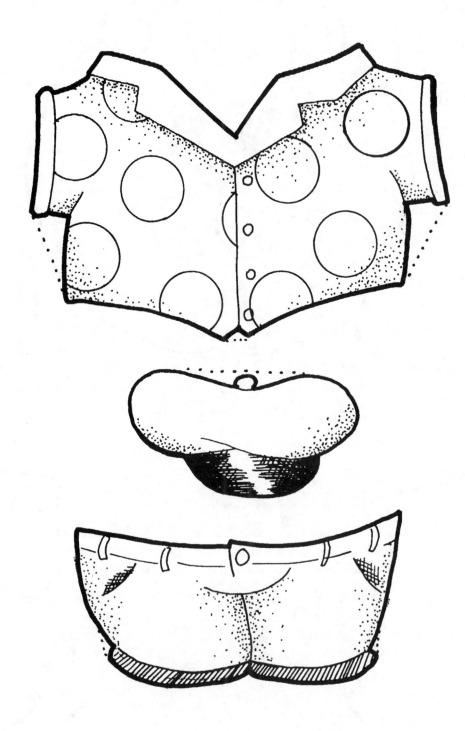

Draw It

1. Draw the pictures.

2. Color.

2  *flowers*

3  *hearts*

4 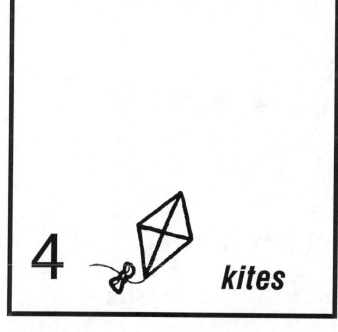 *kites*

5  *balls*

Fancy Pants

Color

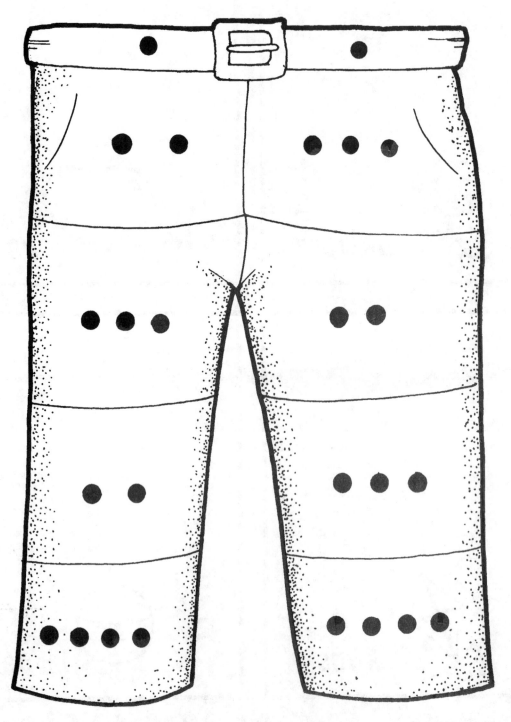

Clothes Matching

Match the jacket to the hat.

91   *#300 Literature Activities for Young Children, Book 1*

All Dressed Up!

1. Connect the dots.

2. Color.

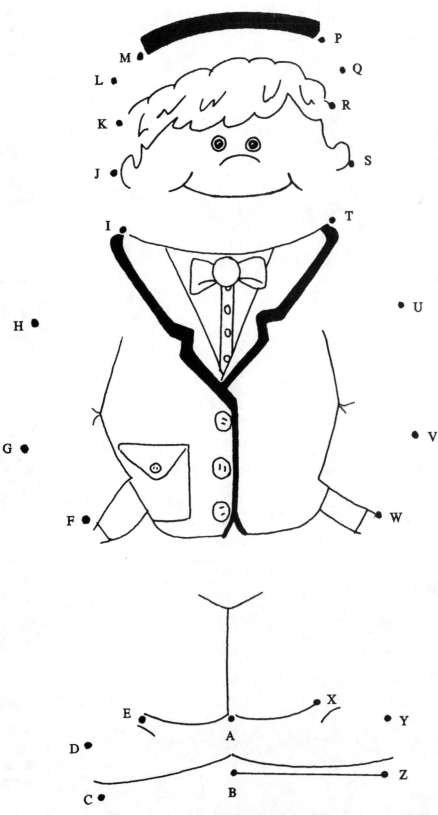

Party Time

1. Color and cut out the pictures.
2. Glue the pictures in order on to a sheet of construction paper.

Match It

1. Match the things that go together.

2. Color the pictures.

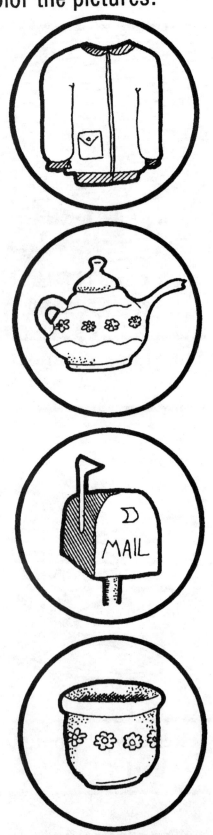

Birthday Cake Pattern

* See suggested activity page 86.

My birthday is: _____

Name _____

Children Pattern

* See suggested activity page 86.

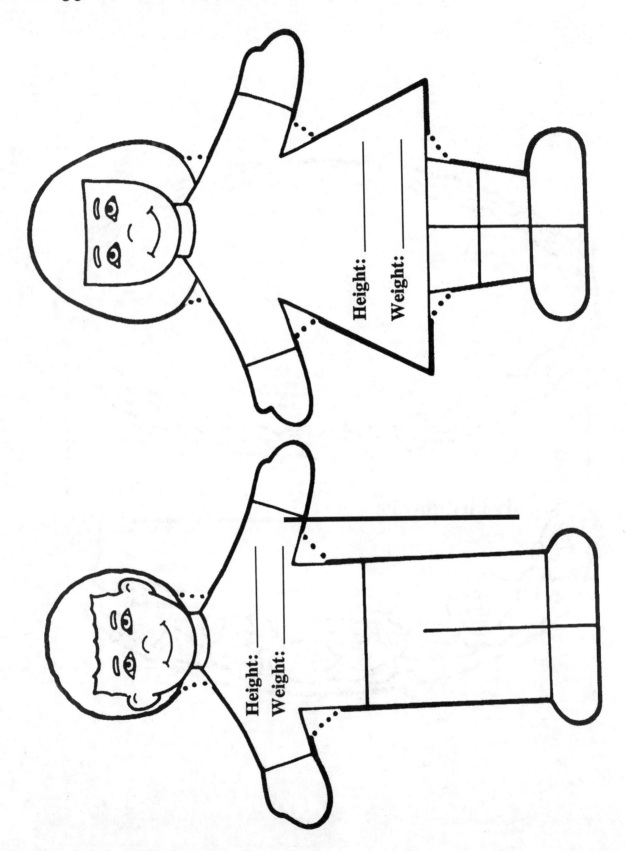

Height: _____
Weight: _____

Height: _____
Weight: _____